The (NEARLY) Teenager's GUIDE to ESSENTIAL LIFE HACKS

AUTUMN
PUBLISHING

Illustrated by Andy Passchier
Written by Carrie Lewis, Megan Lewis and Amelia Lewis

Designed by Richard Sykes
Edited by Suzanne Fossey and Rebecca Kealy

Copyright © 2022 Igloo Books Ltd

Published in 2023
First published in the UK by Autumn Publishing
An imprint of Igloo Books Ltd
Cottage Farm, NN6 0BJ, UK
Owned by Bonnier Books
Sveavägen 56, Stockholm, Sweden

Manufactured in China. 0223 001
10 9 8 7 6 5 4 3 2 1

Library of Congress Cataloging-in-Publication
Data is available upon request.

ISBN 978-1-80108-785-8
autumnpublishing.co.uk
bonnierbooks.co.uk

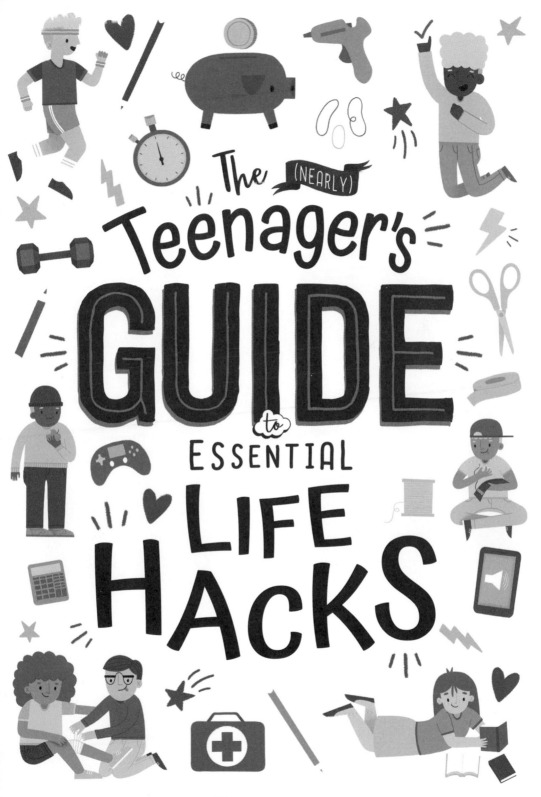

The (NEARLY) Teenager's GUIDE to ESSENTIAL LIFE HACKS

AUTUMN PUBLISHING

CONTENTS

LiFe iS aweSOMe!
(AND OCCaSiONaLLy it iSN't...)

There are two questions in life that are SO BIG that no one ever asks them:

Who will I be?

How will I be it?

And we don't mean dressing up or playing pretend. We mean your very real, and **very important** life. Because life comes with choices: choices about you, how you do your thing in this world,

and choices about how to make the best of who you are and what you've got. Basically, life is **a lot** of choices.

Somewhere out there, a life is waiting for you, and it could be ANYTHING. The world is full of fabulous places and astonishing people. Mysteries. Miracles. Marvels. You will be one of them. See where life takes you: to the tops of the mountains or the depths of your own imagination.

Of course, some people will already be thinking that there's something missing here. What about the dark side of life? What about sadness, death, poverty, and all those other definitely not awesome things that life brings?

Well, yes, every rollercoaster has its

dips, but it's how you **deal** with those dips that really matters. Bad times in life can give you empathy for others and a stronger sense of who you are. Acknowledge your bad times and accept them as part of life. There will always be better days ahead.

You will notice that we don't all start from the same place in terms of making our choices. Some people are born in mansions, or with natural talents and unusual gifts. Don't be blinded by what seems to be other people's advantages though; everyone has something they are great at, and everyone can be somebody. You just need to know who, and how, you want to be. Perhaps some of the ideas in this book can go a little way towards helping you decide that.

So, don't stay indoors watching out the window as the world goes by. Get out. Grab it. Do it. And above all else, HAVE FUN!

a Place For you to Be you

What you have around you can say a lot about who you are. A space that's really yours can also make you feel comfortable and calm. If you can, make a space in your house that really lets you be you.

You might choose a cozy den with lots of cushions around so that you can read for hours, or a shrine to your favorite artist or actor. You might be neat or you might be creatively messy (although moldy plates under the bed is never a vibe). Whatever your style, having a little bit of it around you can make you really feel at home.

Find out what you love

What things do you really love? What do these things have in common? Is it the memories that come with them, or the way that they look and feel? Write down some ideas in each of the sections below.

Things I like looking at:

Things I like reading / listening to:

Favorite colors?

Light or dark?

Old or new?

Favorite texture (e.g. soft, wooly, rough)?

Dull or shiny?

Comfortable, fashionable, or formal?

Now start collecting. Make sure it's possible to be genuinely comfortable either lying down or sitting, because you might want to spend a lot of time in this space.

If your space is your bedroom, try to create somewhere for all the must-haves (like clothes, schoolbooks, sports uniform, etc) so that they don't get in the way. A box in the closet or some under-bed storage is a great way to keep your clutter out of sight. Remember, even if you are "creatively messy," a very messy room can affect your sleep and might even make you anxious if you can't find things when you need them.

Ideas for things you could do:

Photo wall

Download a photo printing app on your phone, and print out some pictures of your favorite people and pets! Stick them to the wall to make sure you see your favorite faces every day.

Shut the world out for a while

Curtains, vines, or string lights? Ask an adult to drape something around your bed for a bit more privacy, or create a squishy corner with blankets and cushions.

Put hobbies on display

Hobbies make us happy, so try mounting an instrument you play on the wall, or framing your favorite sports team's jersey to hang up.

First, find somewhere quiet to be. If you made a place for yourself like on the last page, that will work.

Sit comfortably and close your eyes. Picture a place in your head that you have visited that you particularly enjoyed. It might be from a vacation or a trip to the park. Put yourself in that place.

What can you hear?
What can you see?
What can you smell or taste?
Can you feel the sun or wind?
Is someone there with you?
What are they doing?

happy place

While you are thinking these thoughts and reliving your memories, try to breathe slowly in through your nose and out through your mouth. Breathe deeply, so that the breath goes down to your belly button.

Stay here for as long as you can, or until you are ready to leave.

Another way to keep your head in order is to keep a diary or journal. A diary is a great way to understand your own thoughts. Some people find writing a diary just before they go to sleep each night a great way to calm their thoughts and clear their mind.

me time vs. other stuff

The phrase "organizing your time" probably rings all the boring bells, but before you mentally toss out the idea, take a look at this example planner. Pay close attention to the "reward" column...

	Work	Reward	Clubs	Downtime
Monday	Art homework	Games night		
Tuesday			Football practice	Read a book
Wednesday	Help with cooking	Movie night		
Thursday				Play a video game
Friday	Math homework	Chocolate!	Gymnastics	
Saturday	English homework	Go into town with friends		
Sunday	Clean bedroom	Go to the park		

This planner is one example of how organizing your time well can make your life better. By deciding in advance when you will do your homework or household chores, you also get to choose how and when to reward yourself. Helping out at home isn't just about treats though; it can make us feel good, too! Taking on some jobs around the home shows that you are taking responsibility and growing as a person.

Try creating your own planner on the opposite page. Don't forget to be generous with the rewards. Hard work deserves a treat!

My planner

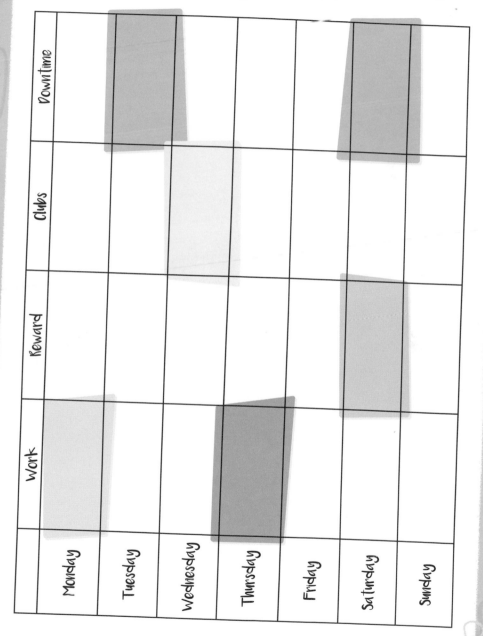

	Work	Reward	Clubs	Downtime
Monday				
Tuesday				
Wednesday				
Thursday				
Friday				
Saturday				
Sunday				

LiFe GOaLS

Goals are very individual and often say a lot about who we are deep down. It's tempting just to think about your work or education goals, but there's lots of other kinds too, like social or fitness targets.

Achieving goals takes time and effort. If you achieve them too easily, then think about setting some more ambitious ones.

Two words to remember are **challenge** and **perseverance**. When you **challenge** yourself, you set yourself a strong goal that will stretch you. **Perseverance** is the effort and determination you need to show in order to get there, including overcoming any setbacks you may encounter along the way.

What's one goal that you would like to challenge yourself with? Now plan how you will get there.

You can have multiple aims, like learning an instrument or saving to buy a new game. Try to figure out a plan for each of them to help you smash them out the park.

Ideas for goals:

Develop a new skill or craft

Run or swim 1 mile

Climb a mountain

Read 50 books this year

Go rafting

Act on stage

Raise money for charity

Work towards my dream job as

....

YOU CAN DO WHATEVER YOU PUT YOUR MIND TO!

Goal:

Are any skills/qualifications needed?

What is the timeline for this goal?
It could be six months for a kindness or fitness challenge, or twenty years for a career challenge!

Do you need help from someone to complete it? If so, who?

What difficulties will you face?

How will you know when you've achieved it?

How will you reward yourself when you've achieved it?

Goal:

Are any skills/qualifications needed?

What is the timeline for this goal?
It could be six months for a kindness or fitness challenge, or twenty years for a career challenge!

Do you need help from someone to complete it? If so, who?

What difficulties will you face?

How will you know when you've achieved it?

How will you reward yourself when you've achieved it?

LiFe ONLiNe

Whether you're a gamer, a watcher, a listener, or just like chatting, your phone or tablet are probably your digital best friends. If you're in the majority, you probably spend a lot of time online.

And that's fine!

But sometimes you have to be smart to avoid trouble and enjoy your time online. Here are some golden rules to follow to stay safe.

Scams

Look out for scams. If it looks too good to be true, then it probably is. This goes for bargains, invitations, offers of friendship, and ads (see page 47 for more information on understanding good and bad advertising). If something doesn't feel right about an email, a message, or a website, click off or immediately delete it.

Personal info

Your personal information is yours and you should protect it fiercely. Pay attention to anything or anyone that wants you to give out your personal information. This includes your name, address, birthday, school, family details, phone number, or a photo. Create a nickname if you're joining a new game or group that you're unfamiliar with.

Do not feed the trolls

Some people feel okay saying nasty things online. But **bullying is never okay.** If anyone makes you feel uncomfortable online, whether it's by teasing or calling you names, stop engaging with them and tell an adult.

Group chats can get out of control sometimes, even between friends. If that happens, don't join in with the person being mean. Instead, reach out to the person being bullied to check

that they're alright, and if you feel comfortable, tell the bully you disagree with them. If you're attacked online, the best thing is to leave the group immediately. But this can be difficult. By commenting less and muting notifications, you can withdraw more slowly, especially if you're worried about drawing negative attention.

Whether it's online or in real life, your safety is the most important thing.

Keep it real

Spending too much time online can mean that you spend less time with family, friends, and on other activities in person. In the long term, this can make you feel unhappy and even depressed because your brain isn't getting the stimulation it needs from other people. Always make sure your life is full of different activities, both real-world and virtual.

Look for the truth

Whether it's fake news or extemely edited images, plenty of what you find online can be false. Try to find sites and follow blogs that you trust are reliable, and stick to them as much as possible. Whatever you are reading or whoever you are watching, remember to ask yourself, "Who is saying this and why?"

Online stays online

Don't arrange to meet up with anyone that you have only met online. If you are really sure you want to meet someone, make sure a responsible adult is present as well. Make sure you meet in a neutral location, and never at your house, near your school, or anywhere you go often.

Report it

Occasionally, we might stumble across or receive explicit content online which can be unsettling. If this happens, it's important to report the content on whichever site you found it (visit reportharmfulcontent.com to find out how to report on social media) and tell an adult about what you have seen, whether it's a parent, carer or even a teacher. But if you aren't comfortable talking to someone you know, visit teenline.org to speak to someone for support. There's always someone to talk to.

DitChiNG DiGital
(FOR a While)

Ditching the phone from time to time and doing other things can be really good for your mental health, but if you've got a big digital habit then it's tough to stop.

Here are three ways that spending too much time online can have a negative effect on you, plus some tips on how to fight back.

FOMO

Fear of missing out. It's what happens when you see what other people are doing, who they are with or what they are wearing, and you start to feel anxious that you're missing all the important events and things that other people are experiencing. Sound familiar? Unfortunately, it can lead to anxiety and depression.

Tips for minimizing FOMO:
❈ Look at what you have, rather than what you don't. This might be possessions, friends, or experiences.
❈ Put down your phone and go and find your friends or family in the real world. You'll soon forget your FOMO.
❈ Some people find keeping a gratitude journal helps. Try to list the things that you are thankful for every day.

Digital Detox Challenge
Want to control your cyber craze? Try this!

Step 1
Name your biggest digital problem or bad habit. Do you do any of these?

- ☑ Doomscroll, or continually look for bad news, especially when there is some sort of international emergency.
- ☑ Wait for the "ping" of new messages and then have to look at your phone RIGHT AWAY.
- ☑ Check who's liked or commented on your posts.
- ☑ Take your phone to bed and chat late into the night.

Naming the problem is the first step to stopping it.

Losing sleep

Constant pinging in the night or losing sleep to reply to messages can stop you from sleeping. Even looking at a screen too close to bedtime can stop your brain being ready to sleep.

Tips for minimizing sleep loss:
✿ Don't take your phone to bed with you. If you need it for an alarm, don't have it nearby; put in on a shelf at the other end of the room so you're not tempted to use it in bed.
✿ Silence all your notifications. Some phones have a "Bedtime Mode" which allows you to set a bedtime and blocks all notifications while you sleep (don't worry, it doesn't block the alarm!).
✿ Try and stop using your phone completely about an hour before you go to bed. This should make falling asleep easier.

Feeling negative

The algorithms on social media mean one thing: the more time you spend looking at something, the more it will pop up on your feed. So, if your feed is full of negativity, the more you scroll through it, the deeper into the black hole you will go.

Tips for minimizing negativity:
✿ If anyone you follow online makes you feel bad for any reason, click "unfollow."
✿ If your feed is filled with sad, depressing things, search for something better. There are lots of "good news" accounts and pages online, filled with uplifting stories and videos.
✿ Click 'see less' as soon as something you don't want to see appears on your feed. Remember: you control your media, it doesn't control you.

Step 2
Turn off all sound and notifications on your phone, including your apps, messages, and emails. This should help you get out of the habit of jumping to attention like a well-trained pooch every time your phone makes a noise.

Step 3
Don't keep your phone with you all the time. Find a place in the house where you can leave it. You know it's there when you need it, but in the meantime, go and do other stuff. You can check in every now and then.

Step 4
When you're ready, try turning off your phone completely while you're at home. Choose one time in the day when you will check your messages and make an event of it. Then turn the phone off again until tomorrow.

COOL BUT CAPABLE

A
re you good in an emergency? Or are you the one running around like a headless chicken, hoping someone with tights and a cape will fly to the rescue?

Remember, not all heroes wear capes! A few handy bits of know-how can transform you from chicken to savior, or at least make you helpful in a crisis. Check this list to see how you are doing and what else you could learn.

- I know how to contact all the emergency services. ☐

- I know how to get out if there is a fire at home or at school. ☐

- I know how to prevent fires at home or at school. ☐

- I know how to use everything in a first-aid kit.

- I know how to treat a burn, nosebleed, and minor cut. ☐

- I know what to do if someone faints or loses consciousness. ☐

- I know how to keep someone calm by helping them breathe slowly. ☐

- I know how to cross roads safely and how to help others cross safely.

- I can find my way around by using a map. ☐

- I know what to do when there is a power cut.

FiND YOUR VOiCE

Whether you want to be a historic world leader or whether you just think it's unfair that you have to use the bathroom last every day, it's always good to know how to stand up for what you believe in.

Often, when we speak up for ourselves, we either lose our temper or feel no one is listening.

Follow the **7 Ds** to make sure you stay calm and hold **everyone's** attention.

Do practice what to say

When it comes to persuasion, preparation pays off. The first words that come out of your mouth might not be well-thought-out or come across as angry. Practice by yourself beforehand so you get it right.

Decide what you want

You have to know what your goal is and tell people. Whether it's a meat-free-Monday at home, or to be the head of the student council, say it as it is! Don't be ashamed to want the things you want or think what you think. Often, when you speak your mind, other people will support you in getting what you want.

> *"When you find your voice, you find your power."*
>
> Anonymous

Demand their attention

If you have something important to share, make sure everyone involved is present, and that their eyes are on you. Ask them to put down their phones, and let them know that you are serious about it.

Don't shout: explain calmly

You may feel very passionate or even angry about your point of view. But we all know that shouting never wins people over, no matter how loud we get. It can also create tension and result in unnecessary arguing. If you feel your voice rising, breathe, take a sec, then go again.

Don't complain: *tell people what you want*

Complaining is easy, but changing things for the better takes effort. If you want to change something, like the way the school recycles plastic or how your house deals with food waste, tell people how you think it should be, not just what is wrong. Presenting a solution, as well as an argument, will help you gain more support.

Deep breaths: keep cool

Especially if you get into a long and difficult conversation. Keep breathing and stay calm.

Deliver your point of view

It's good to have an opinion, but other people can have them too. Remember to show respect to other people's point of view and don't be upset if not everyone shares your thoughts.

> **"SPEAK UP, EVEN IF YOUR VOICE SHAKES."**
>
> Maggie Kuhn

FaiL BetteR

Failing at things can be scary or feel bad. Remember though: everybody does it. No one is perfect at everything the first time they try.

One of the first things professional snowboarders learn is how to fall over. If they were to start with the jumps and flips, they might look impressive right away, but the first time they fell, they could break a bone or really hurt themselves. Knowing how to fail first means you're free to try more and more ambitious things.

"Success is sometimes the outcome of a whole string of failures." Vincent Van Gogh

As well as allowing us to attempt bigger, braver things, failure also has a lot to teach us. Lots of scientific breakthroughs happened when scientists made mistakes. When Alexander Fleming accidentally left a Petri dish full of bacteria that he was studying by an open window, it got contaminated by mold spores. Fleming noticed that the mold and the bacteria wouldn't grow in the same place. When he looked more closely, he discovered that the liquid from the mold contained a form of penicillin, an antibiotic. This discovery revolutionized the way modern medicine works and has saved countless lives.

How to fail better

Take a breath and remind yourself that you are still learning. Studies show that making a mistake helps your brain develop new pathways so you can learn more easily.

Focus on the amount of effort you've put in, not on the ultimate achievement. For example, rather than thinking "I wish I'd won that race," try flipping it: "I'm proud that I ran my fastest."

ASK YOURSELF:

1. What can I learn from this?

2. What will I do differently next time?

3. Do I need help?

4. Who can I ask for advice?

Find out about times other people around you have failed, and what they said about it:

"Failure is success in progress."

Albert Einstein

study and skills

Whether you love studying or hate it, we all have to do it at some point. Once you find your own preferred study style, the whole process can be much easier.

Here are some top tips and helpful habits you can build to do your very best.

Eyes on the prize

Feeling motivated is really important when you're starting to study, but sometimes that motivation is hard to find. That's why keeping your eyes on the prize is key. Whether your dream is to work at NASA or to keep bees, studying those subjects will set you on the right track. Picture yourself achieving your goals and how good it will feel, then maybe this first step won't seem so hard.

1, 2, 3 GO!

Some of us need a little push to get started. One way to do it is to make a little routine. For example, sharpening a pencil, getting yourself a drink, then straightening up your pens.

Decide on two or three things to put into your routine, then complete them each time before you study. Over time, your brain will start preparing itself to focus while you follow your routine.

Time management

Decide what you want to study, when you will study it, and how long you'll study for. Take a time-limited break if you need to after every 30 minutes or so. When you have reached your goal, reward yourself properly with something that makes you feel good, like a big mug of hot chocolate, or some time on your gaming console.

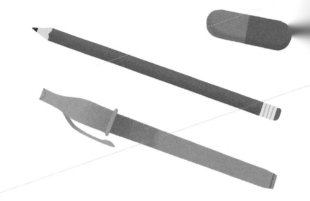

Teach someone else

A really good way to remember what you've learned is to teach someone else. Find a willing listener and tell them all about what you're learning. If they understand and ask questions, then you're doing it right!

Make notes

Writing notes is a foolproof way of ensuring you don't forget anything. But making notes isn't about writing a lot, it's about jotting down the most important bits of information in an easy-to-read way that suits you. Some people use diagrams and mind maps, others use tables or color coded lists, or separate each topic into different exercise books. Whichever method you choose, your notes are for your eyes only, so get creative and find out what works best for you.

"Successful people are not gifted. They just work hard, then succeed on purpose."

G. K. Nielson

FiND YOUR STyLE

Everyone learns differently. What's memorable for you might be totally forgettable for your friend. Figuring out what approach is best for you means that you can use your study time more effectively. Use the quiz below to find your learning style.

1. If you're stuck playing a video game, do you...

a) ... look online for a video?

b) ... read a walkthrough?

c) ... try lots of options until you figure it out on your own?

2. Which of these do you find most distracting when you're trying to study?

a) Watching the view outside the window.

b) People talking loudly outside.

c) An uncomfortable chair.

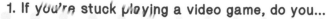

3. What do you like to do most for fun?

a) Read or draw.

b) Listen to music.

c) Play sports.

4. If you're giving someone directions to your home, do you tell them...

a) ... a description of the landmarks they'll see on the way?

b) , the names of the roads and streets they should follow?

c) ... to follow you. It'll be simpler to just show them.

5. When you're bored, are you...

a) ... doodle in your notebook?

b) ... chat with someone or text?

c) ... fidget or walk around the room?

28

Time management

Decide what you want to study, when you will study it, and how long you'll study for. Take a time-limited break if you need to after every 30 minutes or so. When you have reached your goal, reward yourself properly with something that makes you feel good, like a big mug of hot chocolate, or some time on your gaming console.

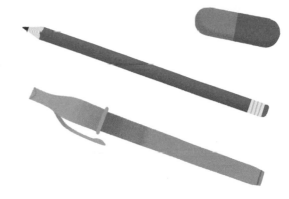

Teach someone else

A really good way to remember what you've learned is to teach someone else. Find a willing listener and tell them all about what you're learning. If they understand and ask questions, then you're doing it right!

Make notes

Writing notes is a foolproof way of ensuring you don't forget anything. But making notes isn't about writing a lot, it's about jotting down the most important bits of information in an easy-to-read way that suits you. Some people use diagrams and mind maps, others use tables or color coded lists, or separate each topic into different exercise books. Whichever method you choose, your notes are for your eyes only, so get creative and find out what works best for you.

"Successful people are not gifted. They just work hard, then succeed on purpose."

G. K. Nielson

FIND YOUR STYLE

Everyone learns differently. What's memorable for you might be totally forgettable for your friend. Figuring out what approach is best for you means that you can use your study time more effectively. Use the quiz below to find your learning style.

1. If you're stuck playing a video game, do you...
a) ... look online for a video?
b) ... read a walkthrough?
c) ... try lots of options until you figure it out on your own?

2. Which of these do you find most distracting when you're trying to study?
a) Watching the view outside the window.
b) People talking loudly outside.
c) An uncomfortable chair.

3. What do you like to do most for fun?
a) Read or draw.
b) Listen to music.
c) Play sports.

4. If you're giving someone directions to your home, do you tell them...
a) ... a description of the landmarks they'll see on the way?
b) ... the names of the roads and streets they should follow?
c) ... to follow you. It'll be simpler to just show them.

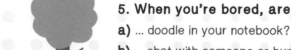

5. When you're bored, are you more likely to...
a) ... doodle in your notebook?
b) ... chat with someone or hum to yourself?
c) ... fidget or walk around the room?

Mostly As:
Visual learner

You learn best by seeing things.

Highlight key information in your books and printouts.

Color-code your study notes and use lots of diagrams.

Make posters and mind maps so you can see how different information fits together.

Your ideal study space is somewhere clear and tidy, without lots of distracting clutter, so you can focus on your colorful notes.

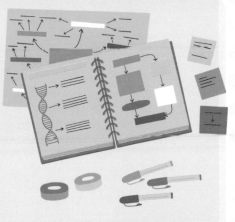

Mostly Bs:
Auditory learner

You learn best by hearing things.

Record yourself reading out your notes and listen back to them.

Use mnemonics, rhymes, or jingles.

Find a study partner to talk things through.

Your ideal study space is somewhere quiet, without too much noise. Use quiet background music or natural sounds to help block out distractions.

Mostly Cs:
Kinaesthetic learner

You prefer a hands-on way of learning.

Make flash cards so you can flick though them while out and about.

Make one of the fidget toys on page 30 to keep your hands busy while watching tutorials.

Test things physically if you can. Try doing an experiment or working with a friend to act things out.

Your ideal study space is somewhere you can pace, walk, or fidget without distracting other people. If you have a study buddy who works the same way as you, that's even better.

Fidget toys

If you have trouble concentrating on your work or sometimes get nervous about things, you might have used a fidget toy. These come in all shapes and sizes, and usually work by calming the mind and helping you to manage your concentration.

Really popular fidget toys include fidget spinners and infinity cubes. Some people also use beads on bracelets, or hair ties. Which have you tried? Did you find it helpful? If you want to try using a fidget toy to help you concentrate, here are some that you can make yourself.

Squishy stress ball

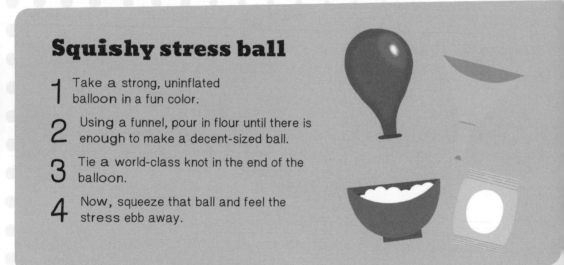

1 Take a strong, uninflated balloon in a fun color.

2 Using a funnel, pour in flour until there is enough to make a decent-sized ball.

3 Tie a world-class knot in the end of the balloon.

4 Now, squeeze that ball and feel the stress ebb away.

Lumpy stress ball

1 Find another strong balloon in a nice color.

2 Fill it with dried peas, chickpeas, or small marbles.

3 Next, tie your infamous knot.

4 Finally, take out all of your stress on your new DIY stress ball!

Fidget putty

Slime is good, but this is neater. Once it's finished, you can squeeze it into all sorts of stress-relieving shapes.

Putty Ingredients:

* 1 cup of flour
* ½ cup of water
* ¼ cup of salt
* Food coloring

Directions:

1 Mix the flour and salt in a mixing bowl.

2 In a separate bowl, stir a few drops of food coloring into the water.

3 Slowly drizzle the dyed water into the flour mixture while stirring continuously.

4 Knead the ingredients with your hands until it forms a nice, smooth putty.

5 Store the putty in an airtight bag or container. It typically keeps fresh and usable for a couple of weeks.

PREPARING PAYS!

Okay, so it's not the most exciting thing in the world, but studying is necessary if you want to do well in your exams.

We've all been there: you already know it matters, but you just can't get down to studying. Here's a few suggestions for how to organize your study stints into short, manageable sessions.

Schedules are your friend

This is a simple example of a month-long study schedule on three topics. Copy it onto a piece of paper and customize it with your own study schedule. Add colors and make it clear and easy to read. Don't forget to include some breaks, days off and plenty of rewards for when you hit your goals!

	Mon	Tues	Wed	Thurs	Fri	Sat	Sun
WEEK1	Topic 1 30 minutes	Topic 2 30 minutes	Topic 3 1 hour	Watch TV	Topic 1 30 minutes	See friends	All topics 1 hour
WEEK2	Topic 1 30 minutes	Topic 2 30 minutes	Topic 3 1 hour	Day off	Topic 2 30 minutes	Go to the movies	All topics 1 hour
WEEK3	Topic 1 30 minutes	Topic 2 30 minutes	Topic 3 1 hour	See friends	Topic 3 30 minutes	Party!	All topics 1 hour
WEEK4	Topic 1 30 minutes	Topic 2 30 minutes	Topic 3 1 hour	Day off	BIG TEST!	Relax	See friends

Start early

Starting your studying as early as possible will mean that you are never in a huge rush. Short study sessions of just 20-30 minutes can be really effective in helping you retain information.

Make a mind map

Mind maps help to highlight important facts, as well as show the overall structure of a topic. They are great when you need to think creatively and can help you to make new connections between ideas. You can decorate them with pictures to help trigger your memory, like this mind map for a history test:

Go high tech

Make some online flashcards to help you remember things. Add pictures as well as words. Make sure you only have one question per card so that your brain can focus on one thing at a time, and say your answers out loud when using them. You might think you sound strange but it can help you remember them later.

Discover your own study methods. The same ones don't work for everyone, so find one that works for you.

DON'T PUT it OFF

There always seems to be a good reason not to study. Feeding the guinea pig, talking to friends, fighting with your siblings... it all takes up time.

You might even think you work best under pressure, and that cramming at the last minute is the perfect way to study. Really, though, these are all just ways of putting off your studying.

Procrastination

The fancy word for putting things off is "procrastination." We all do it sometimes, but it's really important to recognize when you are doing it, so you can stop procrastinating and get on with what you should be doing.

Slow and steady wins the race

Follow the procrastination race to see if you can achieve **focus**. Think about which corners are most likely to make you "crash" into a procrastination barrier, and where you can zoom ahead with your goals and get ahead.

THE STARTING LINE
Identify the best place for you to work and make it your own. This might be a desk or a comfortable chair—whatever works for you!

CORNER 1
If your study schedule seems like a lot, break it into small steps, then focus on only the first step to start with. When you have finished step 1, focus on step 2, and so on. Just take one small step at a time.

CORNER 5
When you finish one work task, decide on the next. It might be helpful to keep a list and cross things off as you go.

THE FINISHING LINE
Congratulations! You have achieved focus and your studying is complete!

CORNER 4
Shut off your phone to avoid reading messages while you are studying. They will still be there when you've finished, and not letting them distract you will give you a clearer head.

CORNER 2
Set some targets. What do you want to have achieved or learned by the end of each study/work session? Decide how much you are going to do and make sure you get there before you take a break or stop for the day.

CORNER 3
Love to work with music on? Make a playlist in advance that will help you get in the mood to get things done!

take care of your health

When you are working hard, it's crucial to remember that your health is always the most important thing.

When you are busy and perhaps even a bit stressed, it's easy to let things like exercise and your health slide.

Fight the slide by playing Good Health Bingo and recharging your batteries. If you manage a full house each week, claim an extra treat of your choice.

GOOD HEALTH BINGO!

Cross off each square as you complete the activity.

Go for a walk in nature	Sleep for 8-10 hours each night	Have some quiet alone time each day	Read a book (not a school book)	Drink 2 liters of water every day
Eat 5 fruits and vegetables every day	Do at least 30 minutes of exercise every day	Spend at least one evening off social media	Try something new	List 3 things you are grateful for each morning
Watch a feel-good movie	Have a dance party (other guests are optional!)	**Free square** Your choice!	Spend time talking with a family member	Do something nice for someone
Cuddle with a family member, pet, or stuffed animal	Eat a healthy breakfast each morning	Stretch for 10 minutes a day	Do something creative	Revamp a corner of your bedroom
Sit in the sun for a while (don't forget sunscreen!)	Play a board game with family members or friends	Eat something delicious	Make an upbeat/feel-good playlist	Create a list of things you want to do this month

Mental health and your inner cave-dweller

It's important to take care of your mental health when you have tests or exams, but in order to do that it's useful to know how it works.

Although they may feel it, exams aren't really scary. Even if we don't do as well as we want to, there's always another day and another thing we will succeed at.

The reason that tests feel scary is because part of our brain is inherited from our ancient ancestors. Our ancestors didn't live in a nice, safe home; they lived in the wild where there were animals and other fierce things that could eat them. They needed part of their brain to be alert to danger all the time, because that was the only thing that kept them from being eaten.

You have the same brain as your ancestors, but what you don't have is a world full of scary, wild animals. This means that the part of your brain that wants to protect you from mammoths and saber-tooth tigers will start to overreact when faced with any kind of threat.

Now, an exam doesn't have teeth or claws, or a loud roar, but if you worry about failing a test or not being good enough, your body will begin to sense that you feel threatened, and the cave-dweller in you will prepare to pick up its spear and fight, or run the other way. This is called "fight or flight" and it's how humans through the ages have dealt with threats. To calm down your fight or flight response, try to remember to keep some perspective: can a test eat you? No. If you don't do well, then you might not feel great for a day or two, but there will always be another chance to improve.

You don't have to be perfect. Cave-dweller or not, you're still human!

Your phone can't operate on an empty battery, and neither can you!

PREPARING FOR a BiG Day

Big days come in all shapes and sizes. It could be an important football game, the opening night of your dance show, a music exam, or a school test. Whatever it is, it's good to know how to get your head in the game.

The day before

It's easy to feel a few jitters before a big day. If you feel nervous, just remember some positive self-talk. You have done your practice and preparation, learned your lines, and finished your studying.

Now, picture how it will feel to succeed. Close your eyes and imagine how it will feel when you begin. How will you stand or sit? What will you say? What will you do first? If possible, give yourself permission to enjoy yourself. This is the moment when you show other people just what you can do. That's not something to be afraid of, it's something to celebrate!

The night before

Pack your bag before you go to bed so that you're not worrying in the morning. You need a good sleep before a big day, so avoid too much sugar in the evening, and turn off screens well before your bedtime so they can't disrupt your sleeping pattern.

Try to have an early night. As you go to sleep, picture how well you will do tomorrow. If you're struggling to sleep, calmly go over each step in your head until you know it back to front. If you find yourself panicking, read a few pages of a book or listen to some music for a few minutes.

In the morning

B.R.E.A.K.F.A.S.T. Did you get that? Even if you don't normally eat breakfast, it's a very good idea to start, because you're going to need all that extra energy to get through the day.

Again, avoid too much sugar, even though it will give you lots of energy, since you'll crash and feel sleepy as soon as it's worn off. If you can, eat some protein (like eggs) or something that will give you energy for a long time (like oatmeal). These will keep you going for a while.

Pack a snack for later. You might need a pick-me-up before your event, or something to keep you going afterwards when all the excitement is over.

Seeing it through

Try to set off early. If you leave yourself plenty of time to get to your big event, then you're not going to be panicking about being late. Ask a friend or a family member to travel with you so you'll have someone to calm you down and distract you if you start to panic.

If it's a test you're preparing for, they can always quiz you on the way, which will remind you how prepared you are. If you choose to travel alone, take a book or some music with you to keep you chilled out.

NOW, 1, 2, 3, BREATHE... AND... SUCCEED!

MONEY. MONEY. MONEY!

Once upon a time, maybe when you were very little, money was stuff you handed to people in stores. It clinked. It folded. Sometimes it even glittered.

These days, we don't see real money often; it's just plastic cards and numbers on a screen... but that doesn't mean it's any less real. In fact, it's very real and it matters a **lot**.

Often, the first ideas we have about money are from grown-ups. You might overhear them talking in the kitchen about how big the bills are or how much everything has gone up. You have probably learned to tune this out as boring stuff you don't need to know. That's true for now, but soon—much sooner than you think—you **will** need to know, and it's a good idea to know how to manage your money from an early age.

Can I have it all? Please?

Although you may feel more interested in saving the whales than having a savings account, the truth is that most of us want more money than we have. This goes for everyone: parents, nurses, teachers, and even rich business people, and famous actors. Most people, even if they're really rich, can still think of something they'd like to buy that they can't quite afford. For most people, when they want to buy something expensive, a little conversation goes on in their head that goes like this:

Me

Wow! Those sneakers look great. I think I'll buy them!

But look at them. They're amazing.

It's not fair! I want both!

Wait. We got sneakers three months ago. We don't need more.

But if we buy these, we won't be able to afford to go out with our friends.

Well, we can't have both, so we're going to have to choose...

Also me

Time to prioritize

Prioritizing is a fancy way of saying that you manage your money choices in order to get what you want or need the most. But that may mean that you have to give up something else. One way to figure out what's most important is to ask yourself a series of questions:

I want sneakers AND a night out with friends. Can I afford both?

Yes

No

Yay! Go for both!

Which one do you want more?

Sneakers

A night out with friends

Have you got enough money for just the sneakers?

Yes

No

No

Have you got enough money?

Yes

Happy sneaker day!

What can you do to have enough money? SAVE or EARN

Have a great time!

Your grown-ups and money

It's likely that you have asked the adults in your life for things from time to time and they have said no. "No, we can't go to Disney World," or "No, you can't have a new tablet." And so on. They are probably not saying no because they really want to, but because they know about other things they need to spend money on, like food or a new washing machine. Everyday things that we don't notice very much can cost a lot of money.

BANK LINGO

When it comes to opening your first bank account, it's easy to be bamboozled by the language. Here's a quick, handy guide to becoming fluent in money.

What is a bank statement?

When you have a bank account, you get a bank statement to show you what you've done with your money. This normally comes every month, and it's to help you keep track of your spending and earning. Money in your account is called your **balance**.

On your statement you'll see the words **credit** and **debit**. These are bank words for **money coming in** (credit), and **money going out** (debit). If you open a **checking account** or a **savings account**, it will show both of these things in a list so you can see what you have spent and what you have put in.

What's the difference between a debit and credit card?

A **debit card** is a card that you use to take money from your bank immediately. It's like cash, but the money on a debit card is always your own. You can't spend more money than you already have.

With a **credit card**, you have an agreement with a bank that they will let you **borrow** money up to a certain amount (say $1000). But the money is **not** yours and will have to be paid back later, usually with extra **interest**, which is the bank's way of making you pay for what you borrow. You can't get a credit card unless you are over 18 and have a regular income or job.

What's an overdraft and is it a good idea?

The money in your bank account is yours because you have either been given it or have earned it. You should only really spend this amount. However, sometimes, either in an emergency or by accident, you might spend more money than there is in your bank account. This is called an **overdraft**. It's better not to have an overdraft if possible because the bank can sometimes charge you extra money for it.

What's the difference between a checking account and a savings account?

A checking account is your everyday account for putting money in and taking it out to spend on things you want or need. As long as there is money in your account, you can use it right away by using your card or getting it out of an ATM. If you are trying to save money rather than spend it, you can keep it in a **savings account**. Sometimes, these come with more rules than a checking account, but they can also have more rewards.

If you wanted to save money for a big purchase, like a phone, you could put money into a savings account. Sometimes, you might have to tell the bank in advance that you want to **withdraw** (take out) the money. However, in return for following these rules, your bank pays you interest.

Dealing with the bank can be really confusing and overwhelming. If you're unsure about something, as always, ask an adult you can trust for help.

What's interesting about interest?

If you keep money in a savings account, the bank sometimes gives you a small payment each month or year for leaving your money with it. This payment is called **interest**. It is usually added as a small percentage of what you have in the account. If you have $100 saved in a bank for one year, an interest rate of 2% will mean that at the end of the year you will have $102. Free money! Check with the bank to see if you can get interest on an account before you open it.

What is a loan?

A loan is when the bank agrees to give you a large amount of money that isn't yours for a fixed period of time, like ten years. You pay the money back over that time with extra **interest**, so the money that you pay back is more than you borrowed in the first place. Loans are only available to adults. This is because you need to have a job and prove that you are reliable so that the bank can be sure you'll pay the money back.

BANK

SAVING

When you know what you want but you can't afford it, it's time to start saving. But how do you do it? Here are some ideas:

Piggy bank

If you get an allowance in the form of actual bills and coins, try not to spend it all at once. Decide on an amount and put that much away somewhere safe every week. A good old piggy bank can be great. If you save just $5 each week, then that's $25 after five weeks. If you keep going on like that, you'll be surprised how quickly the money builds up.

Pre-paid card

These are like bank cards, but money has to be added to the card from another account first. Sometimes adults set these up for children as a way of making sure they don't overspend by mistake. If you have one, you could ask for some of the money to be put into a savings account instead, so that you can only spend what is available to you and the rest is saved. This could be an easy way to budget.

Bank account

If you have a bank account with a card, set yourself a weekly budget. A budget is an amount that you are allowed to spend. If you set yourself a limit that allows you to keep some money in your account each week, it will quickly add up. Before you know it, you will have enough to spend on something that you really want. This is especially the case if your account has interest (see pages 42-43).

Where does it all go?

You've gotten some birthday money **and** you've got your allowance. You feel loaded, and full of ideas for what to spend it all on, then **BOOM**! Suddenly the money's gone and you don't know where it went.

If this sounds like you, then it's time to see what you're really spending your money on. For a couple of weeks, write down what you spend. Did you really want or need everything you bought? If not, then stop buying it. Save the money for something you really want. Use this chart to track your first week's spending

	Food	Fun	Stuff
Monday			
Tuesday			
Wednesday			
Thursday			
Friday			
Saturday			
Sunday			

Think of something you would like MORE than the things you have written above. What do you need to save in order to get it? Start planning:

thiNK BEFORE YOU SPEND

Now you know all about saving, prioritizing, and budgeting, you're ready to spend, right?

Not quite. There's one more thing to consider and that's **value**. Value can be different for everyone, but here are a few things to consider:

Brand loyalty

Some people have a lot of brand loyalty. That means when they buy a particular thing, they always buy the same brand, whether it's a cell phone or sneakers.

Research has shown, however, that people can be just as happy with non-branded or differently branded items when they try them. On top of that, smaller brands or non-branded items can often be cheaper.

So, the next time you plan to get a new t-shirt or a new pair of jeans, consider a non-branded alternative. Do you really need to spend all that money on a brand name? Or can you spend half as much and be equally happy?

Second-hand is not second best

Whether it's online or in the store, there are plenty of ways to buy clothes, shoes, and other things second-hand. If you can get what you want for less money by looking through some second-hand shops, what's not to like?

Buying second-hand can also be a great way to show how creative you are and stand out from your friends.

Outlet stores

If you really like a particular store, then see if you can track down an outlet store or factory store. Sometimes these have great offers if you keep looking.

Need vs. want

Everyone's needs are different. If you are serious about sports, you probably shouldn't buy the cheapest shoes or uniform. You might find that one brand does work best for you and that's fine. However, if you're not sure if you'll still be doing it in a month, then you need to ask yourself if you really need to spend the money or whether there's something better down the line.

It's the same with tech—does a new tablet or phone really do more than your old one? Maybe there's a better way to get what you want.

Before you buy anything, ask yourself:
DO I REALLY NEED IT?

Advertising–is it good or bad for you?

We probably see hundreds of ads every day. Whether it's on TV, YouTube or through social media influencers. These can seem useful, since they keep us informed about new products or services that can be good for us, but ultimately, ads have one job: to persuade you to part with your cash. So, it's a good idea to know how ads work, otherwise you might end up buying things that you don't really need or want. You need to build your advertising immunity, because ads have very particular ways of persuading us.

What are you anxious about?

Sometimes it's as if an advertiser can read your thoughts and knows what worries secretly haunt you in the night. Is my skin good enough? Am I using the right deodorant? Does my hair look okay? Advertisers know that people worry a lot about their appearance, so the wording of an ad can often reflect these worries—even when you have **nothing** to worry about in reality.

Look out for phrases like these in ads:

A big part of advertising is to play on what's called "social anxiety." Social anxiety is what happens when you feel you are missing out in some way. Advertising sometimes makes you feel that everyone has tried a new product except you.

Have YOU discovered...?

Want to know the secret of...?

Everyone's talking about the new...

One good way to build your advertising immunity is to get really good at seeing these phrases for what they are. Is it meant to make you anxious, and if so, why? Do you really need to improve in this way? Probably not. If so, beat the advertisers at their own game and just ignore them.

Try this: each time you read an ad, change the product to something silly, like cow horns, a curly tail, or a silver wig!

Are you worried about your...?

Still using your old...?

Concerned about...?

FLASH SALE!

BUY NOW!!

LAST CHANCE

MaKiNG MONeY

One easy way to earn cash might be to do jobs for friends or family. Here are some money-making ideas to give you some spending power:

Cleaning

Lots of busy families, or people who struggle to move around, may need help with their cleaning. This can work well as you can schedule it to suit yourself. However, just remember that cleaning does have to be done properly: you can't skip the gunky drain just because it's gross!

Car wash

You could start with family cars and move onto friends when you have perfected your buffing. All you need is a bucket, a source of water, and a sponge or towel. Be prepared to get soaked!

Dog walking

Good with animals? Then this is an enjoyable way to get some extra cash. But remember, dogs are a serious responsibility, so if you're offering to provide care you must be prepared—pooper scooper and all!

Landscaping

If you like the outdoors then this could be the perfect job. It's a great excuse to get some fresh air and a bit of exercise in, too.

Babysitting

If you have younger relatives then this should be a piece of cake- although your little cousins and siblings may just see you as a big playmate and not an authority figure when it's time for them to go to bed...

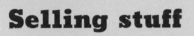

Selling stuff

One good way to get extra cash is to sell your old things, like books, games, and clothes. There are plenty of websites and apps to help you with this. Just be careful of who has access to your personal information when you are selling.

Safety & support

If you are doing a job, make sure that it's safe and that you are comfortable with what you are asked to do. You should always be given proper information, equipment, and support for any job. If you are babysitting for a family friend, make sure you are given emergency contact numbers, told where the first-aid kit is, and given a basic set of instructions to follow. If you are cleaning, make sure you are told what to clean and what products to use. Remember, it's hard to do a job well if you are not told how to do it.

What other money-making ideas can you think of? Make a list below:

iS YOUR hOBBY a GOLDMiNE?

Has someone described you as an "enterprising entrepreneur" or a "talented tycoon?"

Well, the answer to your financial prayers might already be at your fingertips—especially if you're the next Pablo Picasso. But even if you're not, you might be able to turn your favorite craft or pastime into cash.

Crafting is not only good for your bank balance but for your mental health, too. It can help you relax and be less anxious. So, if you've been meaning to learn to knit, why not start now?

Jewelry making

If you love to make things with beads and charms, why not set up a jewelry store online or at a craft fair? Do some trend-spotting and experiment with different styles to create a distinctive character to your work.

Bracelets tend to use fewer beads than necklaces, so you could start with those and see where it leads. If you're allowed, why not wear some of your pieces to school and see if your friends and peers start asking where you got them.

Finger puppets

If you know how to knit, why not try making some small children's gifts and toys? These are quick to make and will look good when you sell them. Who can resist a little knitted finger-kitten?

If you're a whiz with the knitting needles, or the crochet hook, you could make themed sets: five farm animals, or five jungle animals. Find a fun way to display them and people will snap them up as gifts.

Christmas crafts

Christmas is a great time to sell your wares, and Christmas-themed crafts will be popular, too. You could make cards or gift tags to sell individually or in packs. You might even make stockings or tree decorations out of felt.

You and some friends could go together and find a local Christmas craft fair where you can rent a booth. Each agree to make a different craft so that there's no crossover, and decide beforehand how you're going to split the profits!

Candle making

Candle making can be a relaxing pastime as well as a way to make money. If you look in the stores, you'll see that candles can be  pricey but people still buy them. You can make them yourself really easily with a few supplies and a little bit of know-how.

Ask family and friends to collect empty jars for you. Then, when you have all your equipment, experiment with colors, scents, and styles to see what works. Give a few away as gifts and see what people think. Once the rave reviews start pouring in, you can sell your candles online or at craft fairs.

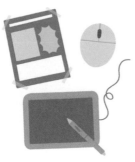

Design skills

Are you a budding graphic or web designer? Do you have a good eye for colors and layout? Put your skills to good use designing posters and flyers for local businesses, or building websites for your friends and family.

Remember to save a copy of your designs. That way, if you decide to become a graphic designer when you're older, you'll be able to put them into your portfolio when you apply to design school.

Born to perform

If you can play music, why not join up with others and perform at some local events? Play for a party or a local show. You could even record your own music and release it online.

Street performing is a rite of passage for many musicians, and it can be a good space to develop ideas and try new material. However, you can't just show up and start playing. You'll need to check with local government about where and when you can set up, and you might need to apply for a license. Ask an adult to help you find out all the details, and if you do start street performing, make sure you have an adult nearby during your performances.

If music isn't your thing, what about a magic show? If you're good at doing card or magic tricks, you could put on a show and charge an entrance fee.

Photography & film-making

If you have an eye for a good image, why not take some photos and get them printed? People love to see pictures of nature, or things taken from an interesting angle.

You could also offer to video family events or parties. Videos are a great keepsake. Practice your filming technique around the house before you try it for money.

Let's Fix it

Which of these can you do?
- ☐ Sew on a button
- ☐ Mend a sock
- ☐ Patch a hole
- ☐ Repair a hem

Fast fashion

You might have heard the phrase "fast fashion" used in the news—but what actually is it?

Fast fashion is when people buy lots of clothes cheaply, wear them once or twice, and then get rid of them again. This is bad for the planet for several reasons:

- ✽ Making material uses lots of energy. The fabric used for clothes has to be grown (e.g. cotton, wool) or manufactured (e.g. nylon). This takes a lot of energy and resources like water, which could be used for something else.

- ✽ Transporting clothes affects the climate. A lot of new clothes are transported around the world in large shipping containers and semi-trucks, which need a lot of fuel and are very polluting.

- ✽ Lots of clothing choice = lots of waste. When clothes are not wanted and are thrown away, lots of them end up in landfill, which is not only a massive waste but also pollutes the planet.

- ✽ So, when we look at the whole process —wasting energy and resources, plus wasting fuel for transport, plus creating landfill—your "cheap" t-shirt starts to look quite expensive for the planet if you only wear it twice!

Ways to avoid fast fashion:

1 Buy fewer clothes and keep them longer.

2 Buy things you really love, even if they cost a bit more. Mix things up by trying them in different combinations.

3 Consider buying second-hand. Scout out your local thrift stores, or look out for nearby vintage clothing sales. You'll definitely pick up a bargain.

4 Find a fix. Learn to repair your clothes, or alter them to suit the way you want them to look.

Make your own

Rather than buying something new, why not try customizing your clothes when you get bored with them?

You could try:

Tie-dye or changing the color of something using clothing dye.

Sewing on buttons in a shape or letter.

Sewing on patches or other shapes.

Tie-Dye

Here's a quick guide to creating your very first tie-dye project!

You will need:

* A clear workspace
* Clothing dye kit
* An old, pre-washed t-shirt
* A bucket to put the dye in
* Rubber bands
* A plastic bag
* Gloves—no one needs blue fingers!

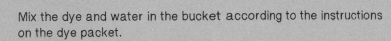

1. Mix the dye and water in the bucket according to the instructions on the dye packet.

2. Check the instructions on the dye packet and see if your t-shirt needs to be dry or wet. If it needs to be wet, soak it in water and then wring it out as much as possible.

3. You can find lots of funky dye patterns on the internet, but to create a basic spiral, lay the t-shirt out flat. Pinch it in the middle and hold onto that small section while you twist the t-shirt clockwise. The t-shirt should fold like a cinnamon roll.

4. Secure the t-shirt with 3 rubber bands, criss-crossing them over. The tighter you wrap the rubber bands around the t-shirt, the more white areas there will be.

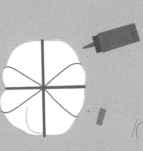

5. Apply your dye to every other "wedge" created by the criss-crossing rubber bands.

6. While it's still wet, wrap the dyed fabric in a plastic bag. The longer you leave it in the bag, the stronger the colors will be. Check the dye packet to see what it recommends, but you can always leave it longer if you want it to be more vibrant.

7. When you are happy with the color, remove the t-shirt from the bag and rinse it in cold water until the water runs clear. Once the rinsing is done, remove the rubber bands and hang your new shirt out to dry! There may still be small amounts of dye that come out of your t-shirt, so for the first few times it's important that you wash it separately from other clothes.

it's YOUR LiFe

It's that question you always get from an extended family member at gatherings: "What do you want to be when you grow up?" If your answer is "Ummmm, I don't know," then congratulations— you're normal.

It can be good to keep your options open as long as possible, but it's also good to have an idea of what you love to do and what you're good at. Advice from family and friends is awesome, but you should be the main decision-maker.

Use this space to write down some ideas and figure out where you might take your next step. You don't have to have your future mapped out (but well done to you if you do!), so don't worry if these are just random ideas. They're a start, and that's what counts.

I CAN BE...

Teacher?

Musician?

If you have an idea of what you want to be but you're not sure, it's okay to dip your toe in and find out. You can do this through work experience or volunteering.

Want to be a writer? Enter a short story competition. Interested in fashion? Get a weekend job in a clothing store. Want to work with children? Ask if you can help out at your nearest Scouting troop, or day camp.

Camera operator?

TV reporter?

... ANYTHING!

EXPLODE YOUR COMFORT ZONE

When it comes to you and your future, don't let anyone else decide your limits for you!

Go and find them for yourself. We all have our comfort zones, but getting outside of them opens up great oppurtunities to really challenge yourself, test your limits and grow as a person. A little bit of discomfort is inevitable! But remember not to put yourself in any danger, act recklessly, or do something that could harm yourself or others.

The next part of this book is all about breaking outside of your comfort zone and trying something new. You can start by putting some ideas in these boxes about where to go next.

The next thing I need to find out about is...

My next adventure will be...

My next act of
kindness will be...

The next thing
I make will be...

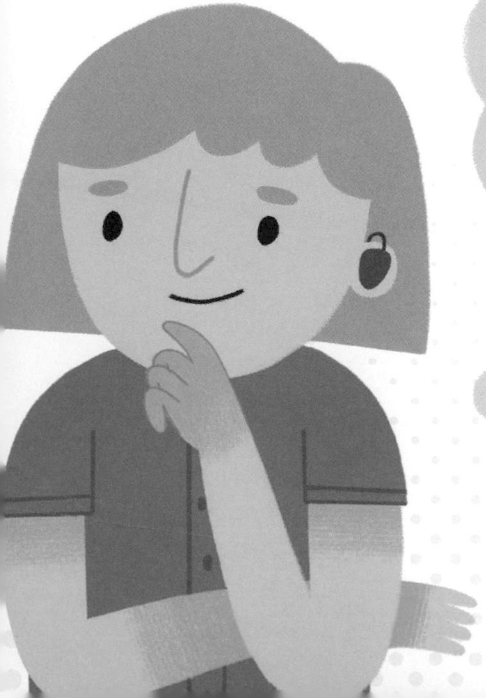

LET'S GET CREATIVE

Getting outside of your comfort zone is a great way to learn new skills and flex your creative muscles. These are some ideas to challenge the way you think and help you get more creative in your future ideas.

Change your routine

You may not think you can do things differently in your day, but you can. For example, if it's safe to do so, go for a walk super-early in the morning. Do some stretches before bed every night. Try meditating. Learning new habits can give you different ways of thinking and open you up to new experiences.

Change your media

Let's start your comfort zone workout with social media. What do you usually look at, read, or watch? Close that. Now, try something different. Look at a news channel that you've never watched before. Buy a magazine. Read a book by an author you've never tried. Listen to a new radio station. What do you like or not like about your new choice? Has it made you think differently about anything? What will you try next? Whatever your source, always make sure it's one you can trust!

Do some journaling

Writing honestly about your thoughts can give you a better understanding of how your mind works. If you keep worrying about the same things all the time, you might be able to write your way to a solution by reflecting on the problem. Focusing on what you are grateful for can also be helpful.

Another way to use a journal is to draw a mind map. Put your problem in the middle of the page. Draw lines out from it to potential solutions. So, if your problem is "I am worried about an exam," one solution might be to set up a study group with friends. Here's an example of another mind map you could draw.

Write a list of places that are comfortable to work in:

Make a list of concentration-friendly drinks and snacks:

Get drinks and snacks at hand

Find somewhere more comfortable to work

PROBLEM:
I don't concentrate very well.

Turn off social media when working

Make a playlist of songs that help you concentrate:

Have a playlist ready

SOLUTION:
Super concentration skills!

SUPER SLEUTH

e said at the start that this book is about choices. But it's impossible to make good choices unless you have good information about what the options mean and where they'll lead. To find good, reliable information, you need to put on your best Sherlock hat and go sleuthing.

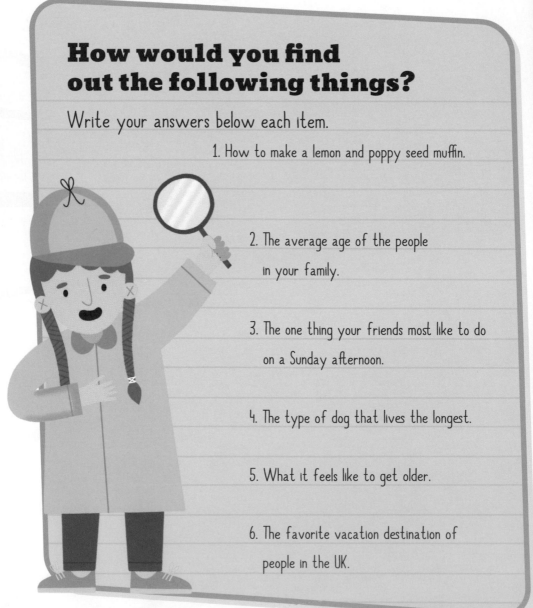

How would you find out the following things?

Write your answers below each item.

1. How to make a lemon and poppy seed muffin.

2. The average age of the people in your family.

3. The one thing your friends most like to do on a Sunday afternoon.

4. The type of dog that lives the longest.

5. What it feels like to get older.

6. The favorite vacation destination of people in the UK.

Internet sleuthing

Obviously, the internet is the biggest source of factual information, but it comes with warnings:

Not everything is correct

The internet is amazing because it's so easily accessible by everyone. However, that also makes it very easy for anyone to share fake information, or manipulate the information that's already out there. It's not always easy to tell good information from bad, so when you're reading an article or watching a video, think about the following: is it too good to be true? Do I know and trust the source? Is the quality of the story good or is it full of typos and mistakes?

Ads are everywhere

Some things are put there by advertisers. Even if an article or information doesn't look like an ad, it may have been put there by someone who wants to persuade you to a certain viewpoint or sell you something.

Balanced is best

An article may only give you one perspective, when a balanced viewpoint may be required. This is especially obvious if the article is blaming one specific group of people for lots of problems. If they're using negative language, they're probably not unbiased.

So, how do you know when you've found the right information?

Check the source

First, look at the writer or source of the information. If it is from a large news organization, e.g., BBC, Reuters, PBS, there's a good chance it's accurate (although it might still be an opinion). Likewise with large information sites like Britannica.

Check the writer

If you want information about a person, try to find an official biography page, not an online forum. Put their name into a search engine and see what information comes up about them.

Dig deeper

Finally, you may want to compare two sites to make sure your information is correct. If multiple news sites are sharing the same story, it's likely to be genuine (although even big news outlets can be taken in by hoaxes, so always read and watch the news with a pinch of salt).

Conversation and contacts

When it comes to really understanding experiences, there can be no substitute for talking. If you want to find out what it's like to have the flu, to get older, or to fight in a war, there is nothing like talking to people and listening to their stories. This is really at the heart of how doctors, journalists, and writers collect information.

If you want to find out more about a particular topic, colleges often hold open talks (either online or in person) that you can book tickets for. Check out their websites for information.

Being critical doesn't mean that you can pick on your sister's fashion-sense. It's about beginning to evaluate your information and experiences.

For example, if you think you might have a serious health problem, where do you go for help? Number these places from 1-6 in order of their usefulness, where 1 is the most useful and 6 is the least:

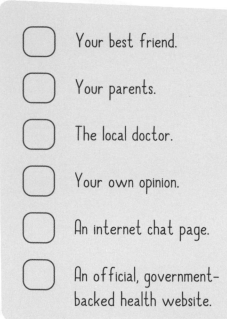

Your best friend.

Your parents.

The local doctor.

Your own opinion.

An internet chat page.

An official, government-backed health website.

Of course, you should always go to a doctor or an official health website, although your family and friends may offer good support. Looking up your symptoms on the internet is not a good way to get a diagnosis, and will probably just cause you unnecessary anxiety.

Now, imagine you have to do a school report about someone famous. Where

would be a good place to start looking for information? Would it be okay just to look in one place?

Write down the name of someone in politics and two places where you can find information about them:

Name:

Source 1:

Source 2:

Now, write down the name of a famous athlete, and two places where you can find information about them:

Name:

Source 1:

Source 2:

Are your sources the same for the politician and the athlete? If they are, that's fine but they could be very different. What you're doing here is evaluating your sources like we discussed on pages 60-61, and deciding if you trust them enough to share the information you found with other people (your teachers and peers).

Being self-critical

From time to time, you might look at what you're doing and think, "I could do better." That's okay. It's good to be able to be critical about your own actions! However, make sure you're kind to yourself too. No one gets it right all the time and you shouldn't demand more from yourself than you would expect from other people.

Also, if you're going to notice the things that you could do better, you must take time to be proud of the things you did well. In fact, make **more** time to be proud of what you did well. In the spaces below, list a few things you could do better—maybe studying a little bit harder, or cleaning your room a little more—and things you do well, like scoring goals on the soccer field, or helping your little brother or sister with their homework.

Things I could do a little better:

Things I do really well:

KiNDNeSS COUNtS

You'll never really understand the impact you have when you are kind to someone, but chances are, they will definitely remember it.

In your list of personal ambitions, how about putting kindness at the top? (Above the movie role and the 5 million online followers.) It might seem like it's a difficult thing to do, but it might be the best thing you can do to change the world for the better.

Why be kind?

Kindness really does make the world go round. It makes people feel better and gets things done. It also makes the person who is kind feel better about themselves.

Sometimes kindness is hard

It can be hard to be kind to people we see every day, even people we live with, but this is really where kindness means the most. It's much easier to be kind to a stranger than it is to be kind to your annoying little brother, or your mom who keeps telling you to do your homework. However, kindness can simply be doing your best to listen or just making someone a sandwich. A little thing can be a big sign that you're trying.

How to begin

One small gesture. That's it. You don't have to solve world hunger on your first day (although it would be unbelievably amazing if you do); you just have to find one small way to be kind. It doesn't have to affect a lot of people; just one is enough. Help someone with directions, or offer to carry someone's heavy groceries, or compliment a friend's new top.

Supporting a charity

One way to be kind is to support a charity. Figure out what matters to you and find ways to support it. Perhaps you could help to organize a fundraising event for the charity, like a food donation day, a cake bake or a sponsored run. Volunteering for a charity is a great way to be kind, and you might meet some new friends along the way.

Random acts of kindness

You might choose to do a random act of kindness. This is a one-time act (although some people do them every day) when you do something kind for a stranger. You might buy someone a coffee, or leave your book on the bus when you've finished it for someone else to enjoy.

Sometimes, people like to "pay it forward." This means that if someone is kind to you, you should pass it on and be kind to someone else. If you do this, then one act of kindness keeps going and going!

What random acts of kindness could you do right now? Write down as many as you can think of in the spaces below. There are a few already written to give you some ideas.

Offer to make dinner tonight

Give flowers to a parent or adult for no reason

Bake a cake for your friend who's having a hard time

Pick up some trash lying in the street

amazingly you

It's okay to have a hero or follow a YouTube star, but you can't *be* them. You can only be yourself. Sometimes, we're so busy looking at others that it's hard to understand and enjoy ourselves just the way we are.

Remember to spend some time being grateful that you are you, with all your funny habits, your likes and dislikes, your kindness, your passions, and your faults. They are all the things that make **you**. Don't be ashamed of any of them. You are unique and you are special. Value yourself.

Identify yourself!

"Identity" is the word we use to describe the way we see ourselves. Although our identity can change over time, it can be really helpful to take a moment now and then to think about it. But identity isn't just one thing, it's a lot of different things (as you'll know if you've seen the Disney movie *Inside Out*).

One way to think about parts of your identity is like skyscrapers in a city, or islands in the sea. Each island is something that makes up a big part of who you are, from your family and friends to hobbies you love, the place you live, or movies, books or games that you're a big fan of.

Imagine that you have five (or more) islands. What are they? Write or draw them here.

Imagine that you are standing on a ship, setting sail among your islands. Where will you go? Who will you meet? What will you do? What will you see that no one else has?

YOUR GOLDEN CIRCLE

So, here we are, almost at the end of the book. We've talked about your identity and your goals, about making the most of yourself as a student and as a person. There's just one missing ingredient, and in some ways, it can be a tough one to talk about. It's your family and friends.

Family

Whether we share our house with one person or thirty people, they are the first humans we really get to know and who, in turn, really affect us. Most families, in reality, are not perfect. They may try to be loving and give you everything you need, but that may not be possible all the time. Everyone is human and your family will experience highs and lows in their own lives. They may have times when they can't care for you well or are angry with you. Most families, however, have a connection which keeps them together, and most people who care for you will try their very best to be there for you. Try to be forgiving when things don't go right, but if things are really difficult in your family or you feel that something is wrong, try to find another adult to talk to that you trust. If your family has problems, they don't always have to be **your** problems.

Friends

The second circle around you contains your friends. You have more choice over these, so try to pick your friends well. The most important quality in a friend is probably trust. You may think that it's being funny or being able to swap clothes, but over time the most important thing is knowing who's really got your back. A friend who won't tell your secrets, who will support you when you need it, and who won't tease you or make you feel bad–that's the friend you want.

Even if it's not perfect, you are surrounded by a golden circle of love. Try to give some back, too.

Others

As well as friends and family, there's a supporting cast of teachers, uncles, aunts, and others. These are in your third circle. Many people, like teachers, are often looking out for you more than you think. Teachers take the happiness, well-being, and the identity of their students very seriously. If they tell you your work needs to improve, or give you a stern reminder about homework, don't take it too hard. What they're really saying is, "I want you to succeed."

RESOURCES

The future can be scary! And it's easy to get overwhelmed by all the different things there are to learn, or to know where to get started.

While asking your parent, carer or an adult you can trust is the best place to start, they don't always have all the answers. So, here are a few helpful online resources you can use to find things out for yourself.

Study

Khan Academy
(khanacademy.org)
Khan Academy is a free K-12 website, covering every topic under the sun, from art to math to life skills. They have a range of courses with videos, slideshows, and mock quizzes to enhance your learning.

Careers

Career One Stop
(careeronestop.org/getmyfuture)
Career One Stop is a website that has lots of career quizzes to guide you towards what jobs might be the best fit for you. It has résumé help, advice on how and where to look for jobs, and can even help you with college applications.

Road Trip Nation
(roadtripnation.com/roadmap)
Road Trip Nation has videos and podcasts featuring personal stories of people in unique career fields. It has quizzes to help you match your interests to different fields, and provides information on how to prepare for that career path.

Money

Practical Money Skills
(practicalmoneyskills.com)
Practical Money Skills helps you learn all about the relevant money skills you will need in order to thrive in the future. Want to learn about how financial institutions work? Budgeting? Getting your first place? Debt? This place has it all!

Biz Kids
(bizkids.com)
With lots of videos and games, Biz Kids is ready to teach you about business, the economy, and adulting in general. It can help you avoid scams, and give you a ton of tips to help you succeed out in the real world.

Mental Health

Kids Health

(kidshealth.org/teens)
KidsHealth covers everything you might want to know about physical and mental health. They discuss ways to help you talk to your parents, and have helpful Q&As that are answered by experts about a variety of things, including driving, hygiene, bullying, and relationships. Nothing is too awkward or uncomfortable to ask here.

Stop Bullying

(stopbullying.gov)
Stop Bullying is an anti-bullying organization that helps adults and children. It provides support and resources for bullying in the home, online, and in the playground or workplace. Visit their website for information and advice on how to contact them.

Teen Line

(teenline.org)
Teen Line is a crisis line for young people. Its website has resources on a range of issues, including dealing with anger, exam stress, and bullying, as well as coping with mental health conditions like depression and anxiety. Their messaging service is led by trained teens who can provide support for whatever situation you are navigating.

iNDeX